Editorial Project Manager
Mara Ellen Guckian

Managing Editors
Karen J. Goldfluss, M.S. Ed.
Ina Massler Levin, M. A.

Illustrator
Kevin McCarthy

Art Coordinator
Renée Christine Yates

Cover Artist
Denise Bauer

Art Production Manager
Kevin Barnes

Imaging
Rosa C. See

Publisher
Mary D. Smith, M.S. Ed.

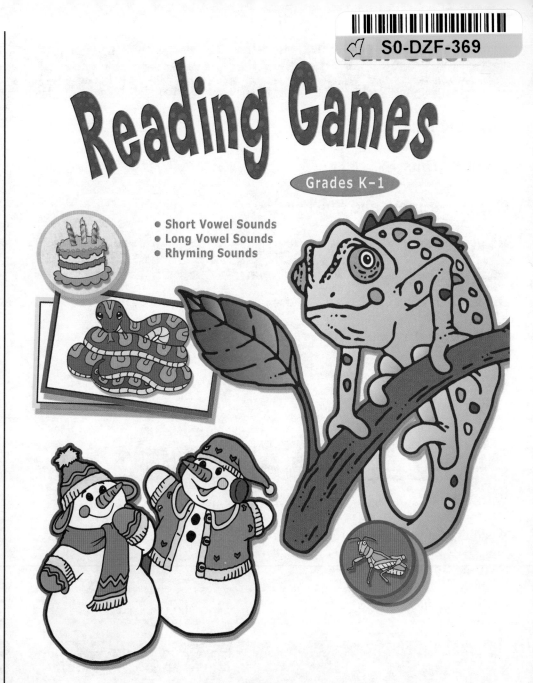

Reading Games

Grades K-1

- Short Vowel Sounds
- Long Vowel Sounds
- Rhyming Sounds

Authors

Bridget Kilroy Hoffman

Julie R. Mauer, M.A.

Teacher Created Resources, Inc.
6421 Industry Way
Westminster, CA 92683
www.teachercreated.com

ISBN-1-4206-3121-7

©2006 Teacher Created Resources, Inc.
Made in U.S.A.

Table of Contents

Introduction

Full-Color Reading Games is a collection of brightly illustrated board games. The games offer kindergarten and first grade students the necessary practice for building important reading skills. These games will help students make associations between letters and sounds. *Full-Color Reading Games* is designed for the creative kindergarten or first grade teacher who strives to provide his/her students with more than just worksheets for practice and review. While worksheet-based resource books are easy to reproduce and use in a classroom, they do not spark curiosity or inspire students. These exciting, skill-building games serve as a powerful and playful alternative to worksheets. Use *Full-Color Reading Games* to facilitate the teaching of fundamental phonics skills and nurture a child's early reading development.

This valuable teacher resource is organized by theme and concept. Each attractive board game captures the attention of students, is relevant to their interests, and develops teamwork. The whole group works together to successfully complete the game. The concepts covered are specifically designed for use with students in the beginning stages of the reading process. Through play, children will practice the following skills:

- Recognizing vowel letters A, E, I, O, and U

- Distinguishing between consonant letters and vowel letters

- Identifying the short vowel sounds of pictures

- Matching the short vowel sounds to the appropriate vowel letters A, E, I, O, and U

- Identifying the long vowel sounds of pictures

- Matching the long vowel sounds to the appropriate vowel letters A, E, I, O, and U

- Understanding the difference between letter names and letter sounds

- Understanding that short and long vowel sounds are represented by the same letters

- Identifying the meaning of rhyming as having the same ending sounds

- Identifying rhyming sounds of pictures.

These colorful reading games are easy to assemble. Just follow the directions outlined in the Preparation section of each Directions page to create great games that can be used in the classroom in a matter of minutes. You determine how your students will use the games, be it in small groups, with partners, as center activities for practice and review, as one-on-one for student assessment, or as take-home practice for family fun. Emphasize that the goal is to work together to fill in the gameboard. (Everybody wins.)

Any way you choose to use them, *Full-Color Reading Games* will provide students with the ability to link sounds to specific letters and master basic reading skills. Incorporate these games into your existing curriculum or share them with parents to use at home. You will be rewarded as your students begin the process of becoming successful lifelong readers.

Helpful Hints

The games in *Full-Color Reading Games* are extremely versatile and provide teachers with multiple options for use in the classroom. The games encourage teamwork. Everyone succeeds.

- *Small group:* Have two, three or four students play together or with the teacher.
- *Partners:* Allow two students to play together.
- *Center activities:* Place the games in a center to reinforce whole-group instruction.
- *Practice and review:* Use all four games on a particular concept with as many as sixteen students at the same time.
- *Individual assessment:* Have one student complete a game independently; then check the game to assess student progress.
- *Family fun:* Send the game home with students for further enhancement of reading skills.

The directions for each of the games are similar. When you introduce one game in the set, students can transition easily to the other games. Students can even teach other students how to play.

> *Note:* It is important to review each set of picture cards before playing a game. Some pictures could be interpreted differently. (Examples—block/cube, tub/bathtub, zig zag/squiggle)

Game Assembly and Storage

All of the games in *Full-Color Reading Games* are easy to assemble. Below are just a few suggestions on how to prepare and store them.

- Using a color photocopy machine, copy the games and keep the original book as your master, OR dismantle the entire book by separating the pages on the perforated lines and copy the direction cards and manipulative pages for future reference. Create each game as outlined in the Preparation section of each direction card.
- Assemble each full-color game board by taping the two pages together. Mount the game board on a 12" x 18" piece of construction paper, oak tag, poster board, or file folder. Laminate for durability.
- Laminate and cut out all necessary game pieces such as flashcards, cover up cards, and direction cards. The cover up cards for each game may be cut out as cards or on the picture outline. (Note: Four additional cover up cards are provided for each game.)
- Store flashcards, cover up cards, and direction cards in resealable snack bags. Label each bag with the game label provided in the back of this book (page 175), and attach each storage bag of game pieces to its game board.
- Organize the entire collection of board games in plastic file boxes, durable magazine/book holders, desktop file holders, or see-through plastic envelopes with button-and-string fasteners or Velcro® closures.

Dinosaur Days

Short Vowel Sounds

Objective: To identify short vowel sounds and match them to appropriate letters.

Preparation

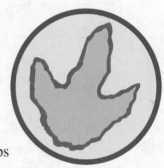

1. Assemble and laminate the Dinosaur Days Game Board (pages 8 and 9).

2. Laminate and cut out the Dinosaur Days Short Vowel Sound Picture Cards (pages 11, 13, and 15).

3. Laminate and cut out the Track Cover Ups (page 17).

4. Laminate the Dinosaur Days Directions Card (page 5).

5. Store the Dinosaur Days Short Vowel Sound Picture Cards and Track Cover Ups in a resealable snack bag. Label the bag with the game name label (page 175).

6. See page 176 for the correct picture card names.

Dinosaur Days Directions

Materials

- Dinosaur Days Game Board
- Dinosaur Days Short Vowel Sound Picture Cards
- Track Cover Ups

How to Play the Game

2–4 players

1. Shuffle the short vowel sound picture cards and place them facedown beside the game board.

2. Divide the Track Cover Ups among the players.

3. Take turns drawing a picture card and naming the short vowel sound. Cover the matching vowel on the game board with a cover up.

4. Continue taking turns until all the vowels on the game board have been covered.

Short Vowel Sound Picture Cards

Dinosaur Days

Dinosaur Days

Dinosaur Days

Dinosaur Days

Dinosaur Days

Dinosaur Days

Dinosaur Days

Dinosaur Days

Short Vowel Sound Picture Cards

Dinosaur
Days

Dinosaur
Days

Dinosaur
Days

Dinosaur
Days

Dinosaur
Days

Dinosaur
Days

Short Vowel Sound Picture Cards

Dinosaur
Days

Dinosaur
Days

Dinosaur
Days

Dinosaur
Days

Dinosaur
Days

Dinosaur
Days

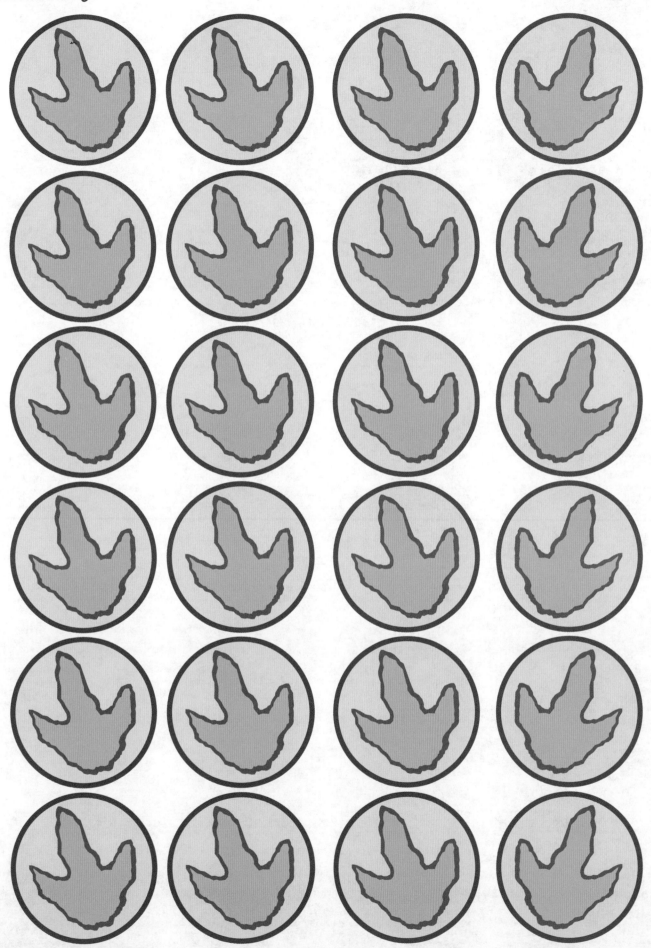

Rusty the Rattler

Short Vowel Sounds

Objective: To identify short vowel sounds and match them to appropriate letters.

Preparation

1. Assemble and laminate the Rusty the Rattler Game Board (pages 22 and 23).

2. Laminate and cut out the Rusty the Rattler Short Vowel Sound Picture Cards (pages 25, 27, and 29).

3. Laminate and cut out the Petroglyph Cover Ups (page 31).

4. Laminate the Rusty the Rattler Directions Card (page 19).

5. Store the Rusty the Rattler Short Vowel Sound Picture Cards and Petroglyph Cover Ups in a resealable snack bag. Label the bag with the game name label (page 175).

6. See page 176 for the correct picture card names.

Rusty the Rattler Directions

Materials

- Rusty the Rattler Game Board
- Rusty the Rattler Short Vowel Sound Picture Cards
- Petroglyph Cover Ups

How to Play the Game

2–4 players

1. Shuffle the short vowel sound picture cards and place them facedown beside the game board.

2. Divide the Petroglyph Cover Ups among the players.

3. Take turns drawing a picture card and naming the short vowel sound. Cover the matching vowel on the game board with a cover up.

4. Continue taking turns until all the vowels on the game board have been covered.

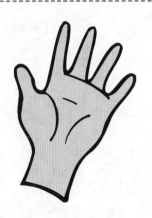

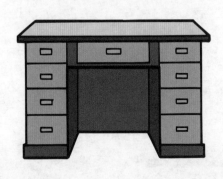

Short Vowel Sound Picture Cards

Rusty
the
Rattler

Rusty
the
Rattler

Rusty
the
Rattler

Rusty
the
Rattler

Rusty
the
Rattler

Rusty
the
Rattler

Rusty
the
Rattler

Rusty
the
Rattler

Short Vowel Sound Picture Cards

Rusty
the
Rattler

Rusty
the
Rattler

Rusty
the
Rattler

Rusty
the
Rattler

Rusty
the
Rattler

Rusty
the
Rattler

Short Vowel Sound Picture Cards

Rusty

the

Rattler

Rusty

the

Rattler

Rusty

the

Rattler

Rusty

the

Rattler

Rusty

the

Rattler

Rusty

the

Rattler

Cool Chameleons

Short Vowel Sounds

Objective: To identify short vowel sounds and match them to appropriate letters.

Preparation

1. Assemble and laminate the Cool Chameleons Game Board (pages 36 and 37).

2. Laminate and cut out the Cool Chameleons Short Vowel Sound Picture Cards (pages 39, 41, and 43).

3. Laminate and cut out the Insect Cover Ups (page 45).

4. Laminate the Cool Chameleons Directions Card (page 33).

5. Store the Cool Chameleons Short Vowel Sound Picture Cards and Insect Cover Ups in a resealable snack bag. Label the bag with the game name label (page 175).

6. See page 176 for the correct picture card names.

Cool Chameleons Directions

Materials

- Cool Chameleons Game Board

- Cool Chameleons Short Vowel Sound Picture Cards

- Insect Cover Ups

How to Play the Game

2–4 players

1. Shuffle the short vowel sound picture cards and place them facedown beside the game board.

2. Divide the Insect Cover Ups among the players.

3. Take turns drawing a picture card and naming the short vowel sound. Cover the matching vowel on the game board with a cover up.

4. Continue taking turns until all the vowels on the game board have been covered.

Cool
Chameleons

Cool
Chameleons

Cool
Chameleons

Cool
Chameleons

Cool
Chameleons

Cool
Chameleons

Cool
Chameleons

Cool
Chameleons

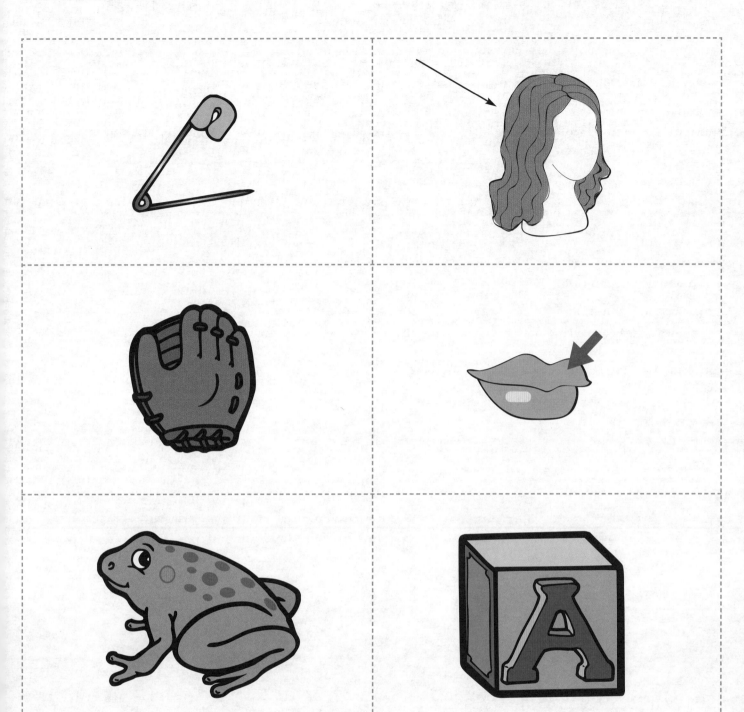

Cool
Chameleons

Cool
Chameleons

Cool
Chameleons

Cool
Chameleons

Cool
Chameleons

Cool
Chameleons

Cool
Chameleons

Cool
Chameleons

Cool
Chameleons

Cool
Chameleons

Cool
Chameleons

Cool
Chameleons

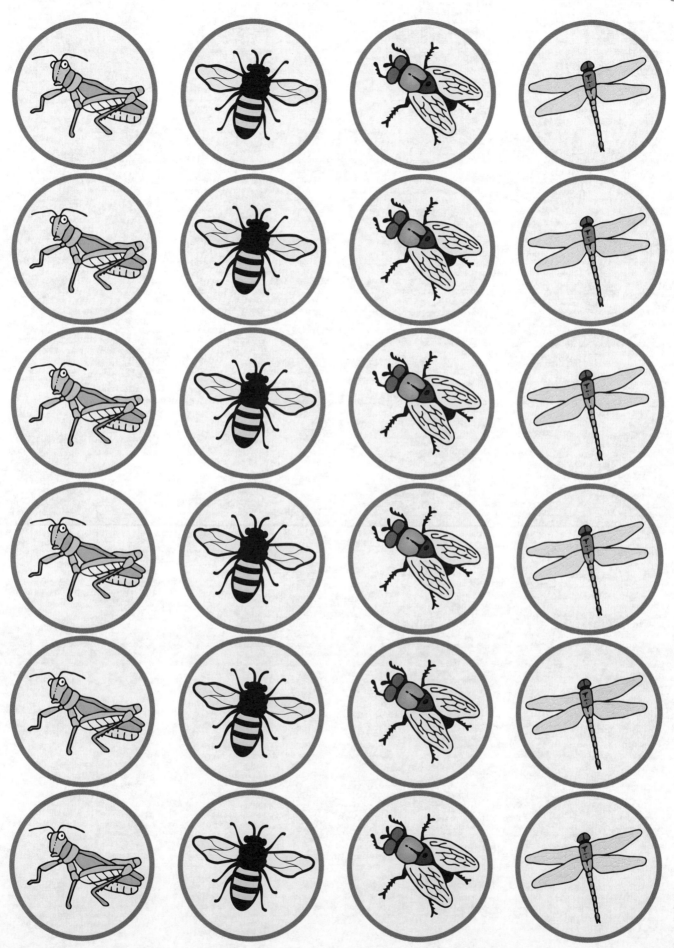

45

Lazy Lizards

Short Vowel Sounds

Objective: To identify short vowel sounds and match them to appropriate letters.

Preparation

1. Assemble and laminate the Lazy Lizards Game Board (pages 50 and 51).

2. Laminate and cut out the Lazy Lizards Short Vowel Sound Picture Cards (pages 53, 55, and 57).

3. Laminate and cut out the Cactus Cover Ups (page 59).

4. Laminate the Lazy Lizards Directions Card (page 47).

5. Store the Lazy Lizards Short Vowel Sound Picture Cards and Cactus Cover Ups in a resealable snack bag. Label the bag with the game name label (page 175).

6. See page 176 for the correct picture card names.

Lazy Lizards Directions

Materials

- Lazy Lizards Game Board
- Lazy Lizards Short Vowel Sound Picture Cards
- Cactus Cover Ups

How to Play the Game

2–4 players

1. Shuffle the short vowel sound picture cards and place them facedown beside the game board.

2. Divide the Cactus Cover Ups among the players.

3. Take turns drawing a picture card and naming the short vowel sound. Cover the matching vowel on the game board with a cover up.

4. Continue taking turns until all the vowels on the game board have been covered.

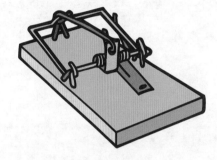

Short Vowel Sound Picture Cards

Lazy Lizards

Lazy Lizards

Lazy Lizards

Lazy Lizards

Lazy Lizards

Lazy Lizards

Lazy Lizards

Lazy Lizards

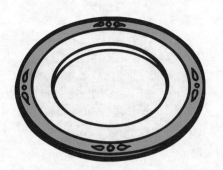

Short Vowel Sound Picture Cards

Lazy
Lizards

Lazy
Lizards

Lazy
Lizards

Lazy
Lizards

Lazy
Lizards

Lazy
Lizards

Short Vowel Sound Picture Cards

Lazy
Lizards

Lazy
Lizards

Lazy
Lizards

Lazy
Lizards

Lazy
Lizards

Lazy
Lizards

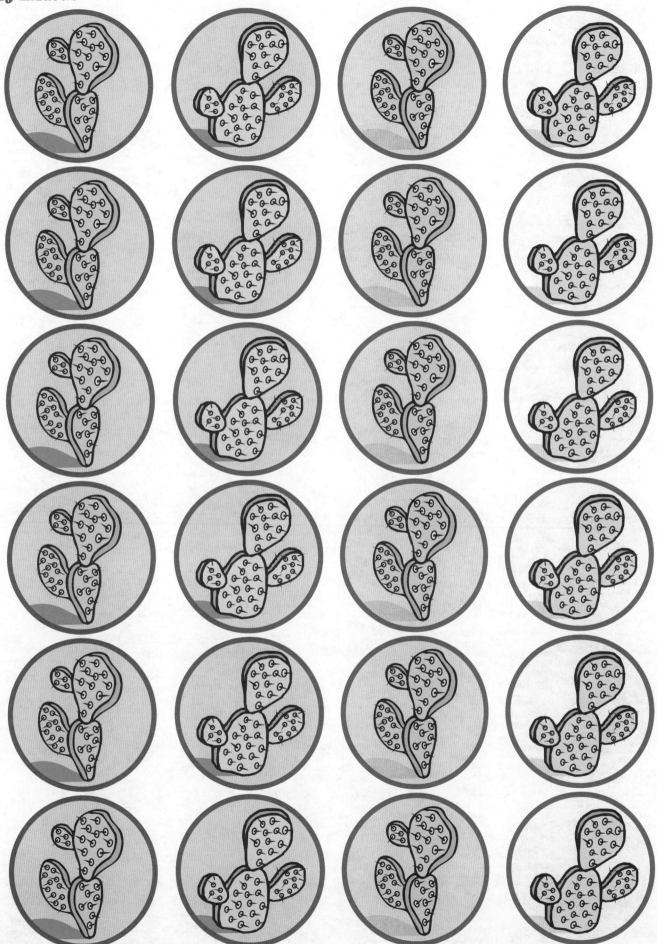

Wacky Wind

Long Vowel Sounds

Objective: To identify long vowel sounds and match them to appropriate letters.

Preparation

1. Assemble and laminate the Wacky Wind Game Board (pages 64 and 65).

2. Laminate and cut out the Wacky Wind Long Vowel Sound Picture Cards (pages 67, 69, and 71).

3. Laminate and cut out the Clothing Cover Ups (page 73).

4. Laminate the Wacky Wind Directions Card (page 61).

5. Store the Wacky Wind Long Vowel Sound Picture Cards and Clothing Cover Ups in a resealable snack bag. Label the bag with the game name label (page 175).

6. See page 176 for the correct picture card names.

Wacky Wind Directions

Materials

- Wacky Wind Game Board
- Wacky Wind Long Vowel Sound Picture Cards
- Clothing Cover Ups

How to Play the Game

2–4 players

1. Shuffle the long vowel sound picture cards and place them facedown beside the game board.

2. Divide the Clothing Cover Ups among the players.

3. Take turns drawing a picture card and naming the long vowel sound. Cover the matching vowel on the game board with a cover up.

4. Continue taking turns until all the vowels on the game board have been covered.

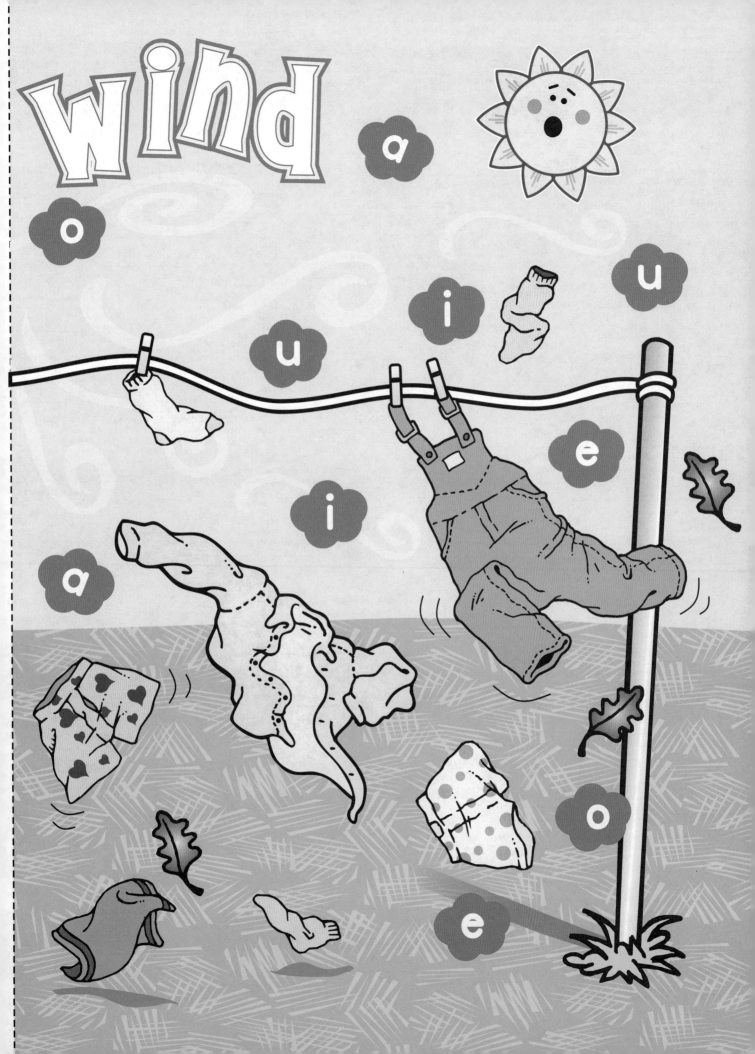

Long Vowel Sound Picture Cards

Wacky
Wind

Wacky
Wind

Wacky
Wind

Wacky
Wind

Wacky
Wind

Wacky
Wind

Wacky
Wind

Wacky
Wind

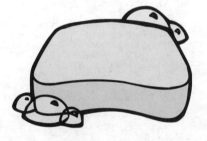

Long Vowel Sound Picture Cards

Wacky
Wind

Wacky
Wind

Wacky
Wind

Wacky
Wind

Wacky
Wind

Wacky
Wind

Long Vowel Sound Picture Cards

Wacky
Wind

Wacky
Wind

Wacky
Wind

Wacky
Wind

Wacky
Wind

Wacky
Wind

Weather Map

Long Vowel Sounds

Objective: To identify long vowel sounds and match them to appropriate letters.

Preparation

1. Assemble and laminate the Weather Map Game Board (pages 78 and 79).

2. Laminate and cut out the Weather Map Long Vowel Sound Picture Cards (pages 81, 83, and 85).

3. Laminate and cut out the Weather Symbol Cover Ups (page 87).

4. Laminate the Weather Map Directions Card (page 75).

5. Store the Weather Map Long Vowel Sound Picture Cards and Weather Symbol Cover Ups in a resealable snack bag. Label the bag with the game name label (page 175).

6. See page 176 for the correct picture card names.

Weather Map Directions

Materials

- Weather Map Game Board
- Weather Map Long Vowel Sound Picture Cards
- Weather Symbol Cover Ups

How to Play the Game

2–4 players

1. Shuffle the long vowel sound picture cards and place them facedown beside the game board.

2. Divide the Weather Symbol Cover Ups among the players.

3. Take turns drawing a picture card and naming the long vowel sound. Cover the matching vowel on the game board with a cover up.

4. Continue taking turns until all the vowels on the game board have been covered.

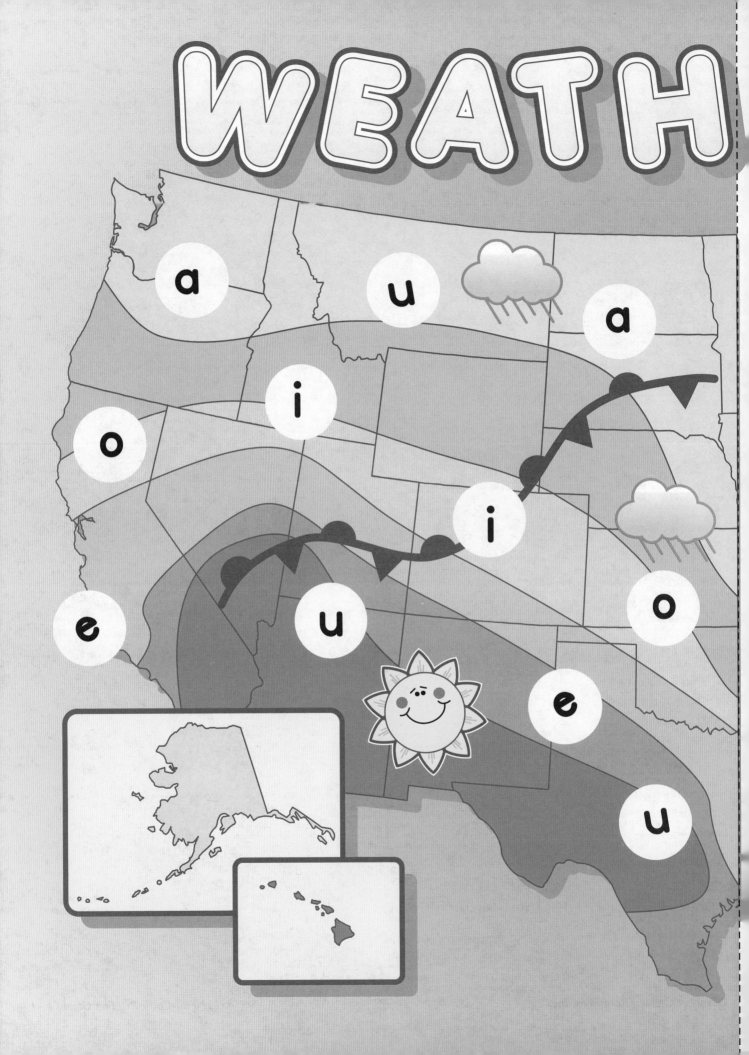

ER MAP

Long Vowel Sound Picture Cards

Weather

Map

Weather

Map

Weather

Map

Weather

Map

Weather

Map

Weather

Map

Weather

Map

Weather

Map

5

9

Long Vowel Sound Picture Cards

Weather
Map

Weather
Map

Weather
Map

Weather
Map

Weather
Map

Weather
Map

Weather
Map

Weather
Map

Weather
Map

Weather
Map

Weather
Map

Weather
Map

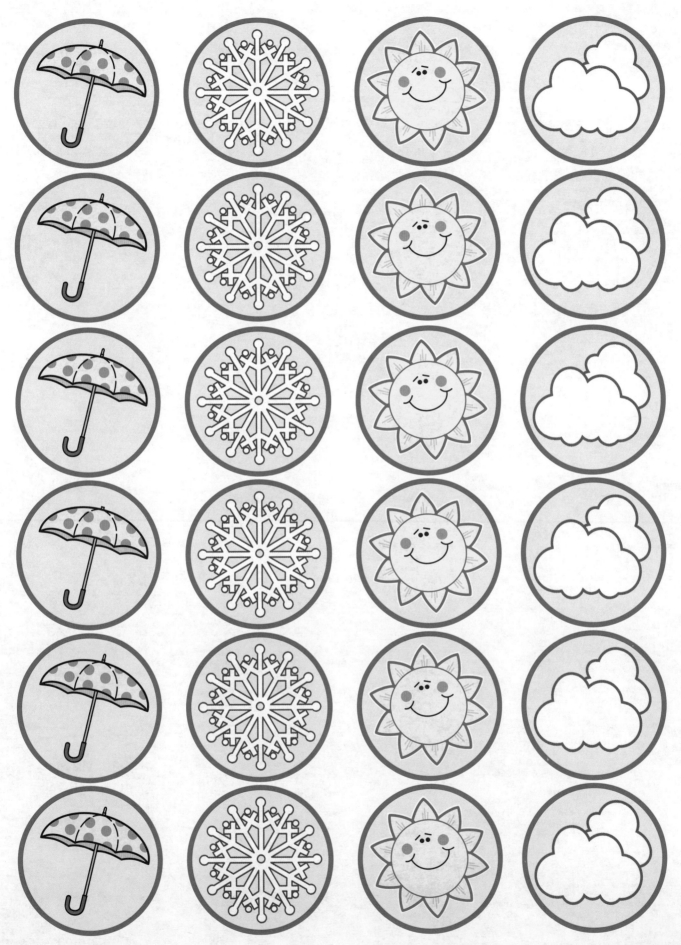

Swirling Snowflakes

Long Vowel Sounds

Objective: To identify long vowel sounds and match them to appropriate letters.

Preparation

1. Assemble and laminate the Swirling Snowflakes Game Board (pages 92 and 93).

2. Laminate and cut out the Swirling Snowflakes Long Vowel Sound Picture Cards (pages 95, 97, and 99).

3. Laminate and cut out the Snowflake Cover Ups (page 101).

4. Laminate the Swirling Snowflakes Directions Card (page 89).

5. Store the Swirling Snowflakes Long Vowel Sound Picture Cards and Snowflake Cover Ups in a resealable snack bag. Label the bag with the game name label (page 175).

6. See page 176 for the correct picture card names.

Swirling Snowflakes Directions

Materials

- Swirling Snowflakes Game Board
- Swirling Snowflakes Long Vowel Sound Picture Cards
- Snowflake Cover Ups

How to Play the Game

2–4 players

1. Shuffle the long vowel sound picture cards and place them facedown beside the game board.

2. Divide the Snowflake Cover Ups among the players.

3. Take turns drawing a picture card and naming a long vowel sound. Cover the matching vowel on the game board with a cover up.

4. Continue taking turns until all the vowels on the game board have been covered.

Swirling Snowflakes

Swirling
Snowflakes

Swirling
Snowflakes

Swirling
Snowflakes

Swirling
Snowflakes

Swirling
Snowflakes

Swirling
Snowflakes

Swirling
Snowflakes

Swirling
Snowflakes

96

Long Vowel Sound Picture Cards

Swirling
Snowflakes

Swirling
Snowflakes

Swirling
Snowflakes

Swirling
Snowflakes

Swirling
Snowflakes

Swirling
Snowflakes

                          #3121 Full-Color Reading Games K–1

Long Vowel Sound Picture Cards

Swirling
Snowflakes

Swirling
Snowflakes

Swirling
Snowflakes

Swirling
Snowflakes

Swirling
Snowflakes

Swirling
Snowflakes

Cottony Clouds

Long Vowel Sounds

Objective: To identify long vowel sounds and match them to appropriate letters.

Preparation

1. Assemble and laminate the Cottony Clouds Game Board (pages 106 and 107).

2. Laminate and cut out the Cottony Clouds Long Vowel Sound Picture Cards (pages 109, 111, and 113).

3. Laminate and cut out the Cloud Cover Ups (page 115).

4. Laminate the Cottony Clouds Directions Card (page 103).

5. Store the Cottony Clouds Long Vowel Sound Picture Cards and Cloud Cover Ups in a resealable snack bag. Label the bag with the game name label (page 175).

6. See page 176 for the correct picture card names.

Cottony Clouds Directions

Materials

- Cottony Clouds Game Board
- Cottony Clouds Long Vowel Sound Picture Cards
- Cloud Cover Ups

How to Play the Game

2–4 players

1. Shuffle the long vowel sound picture cards and place them facedown beside the game board.

2. Divide the Cloud Cover Ups among the players.

3. Take turns drawing a picture card and naming the long vowel sound. Cover the matching vowel on the game board with a cover up.

4. Continue taking turns until all the vowels on the game board have been covered.

104

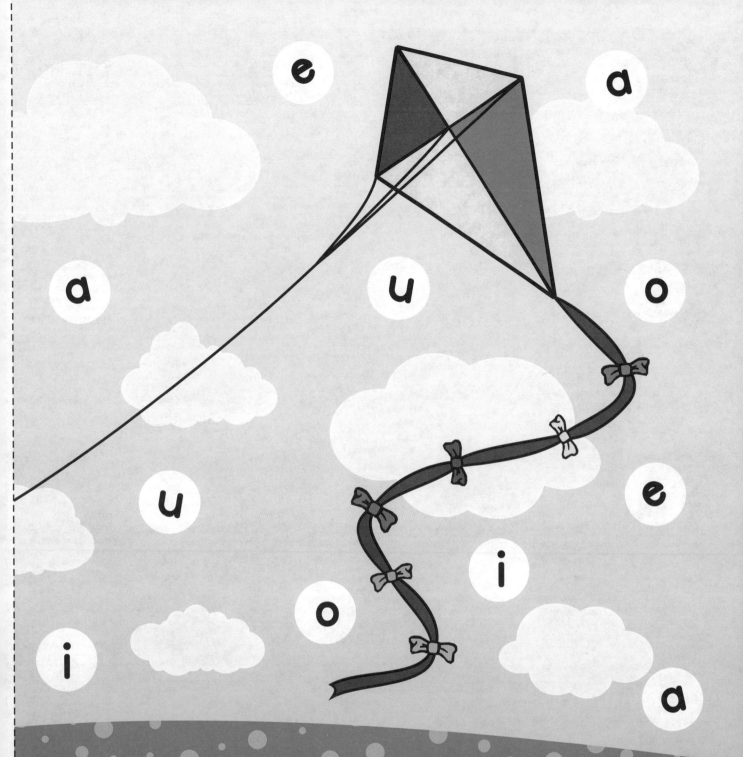

COTTONY CLOUDS

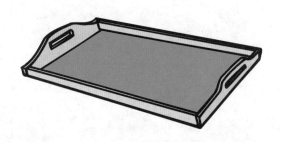

Cottony
Clouds

Cottony
Clouds

Cottony
Clouds

Cottony
Clouds

Cottony
Clouds

Cottony
Clouds

Cottony
Clouds

Cottony
Clouds

Cottony
Clouds

Cottony
Clouds

Cottony
Clouds

Cottony
Clouds

Cottony
Clouds

Cottony
Clouds

Long Vowel Sound Picture Cards

Cottony Clouds

Cottony Clouds

Cottony Clouds

Cottony Clouds

Cottony Clouds

Cottony Clouds

Old Oak

Rhyming Sounds

Objective: To identify rhyming sounds.

Preparation

1. Assemble and laminate the Old Oak Game Board (pages 120 and 121).

2. Laminate and cut out the Old Oak Rhyming Picture Cards (pages 123, 125, and 127).

3. Laminate and cut out the Acorn Cover Ups (page 129).

4. Laminate the Old Oak Directions Card (page 117).

5. Store the Old Oak Rhyming Picture Cards and Acorn Cover Ups in a resealable snack bag. Label the bag with the game name label (page 175).

6. See page 176 for the correct picture card names.

Old Oak Directions

Materials

- Old Oak Game Board
- Old Oak Rhyming Picture Cards
- Acorn Cover Ups

How to Play the Game

2–4 players

1. Shuffle the rhyming picture cards and place them facedown beside the game board.

2. Divide the Acorn Cover Ups among the players.

3. Take turns drawing a rhyming picture card and covering the matching rhyming picture on the game board with a cover up.

4. Continue taking turns until all the rhyming pictures on the game board have been covered.

Old Oak

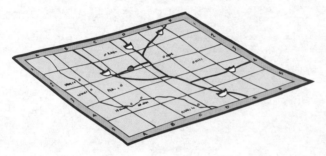

Rhyming Picture Cards

Old

Oak

Old

Oak

Old

Oak

Old

Oak

Old

Oak

Old

Oak

Old

Oak

Old

Oak

124

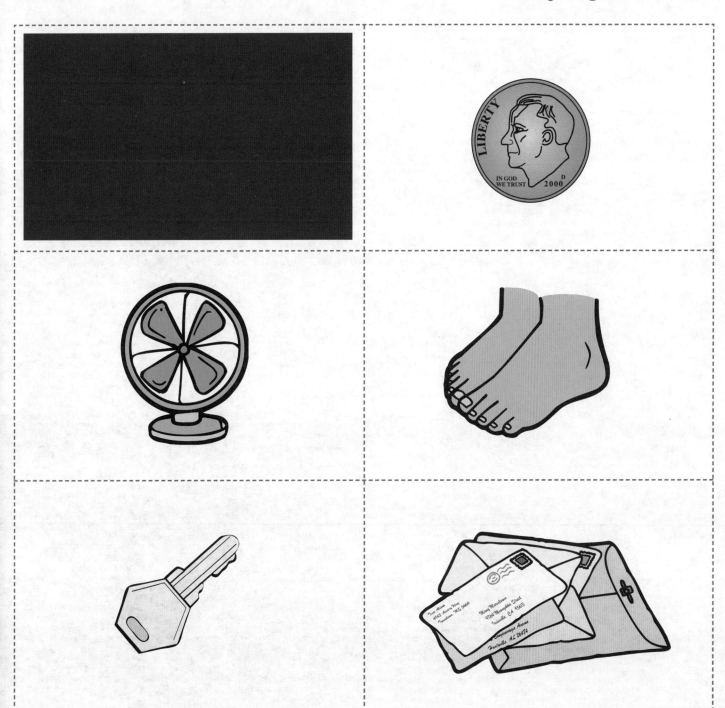

Rhyming Picture Cards

Old
Oak

Old
Oak

Old
Oak

Old
Oak

Old
Oak

Old
Oak

Rhyming Picture Cards

Old

Oak

Old

Oak

Old

Oak

Old

Oak

Old

Oak

Old

Oak

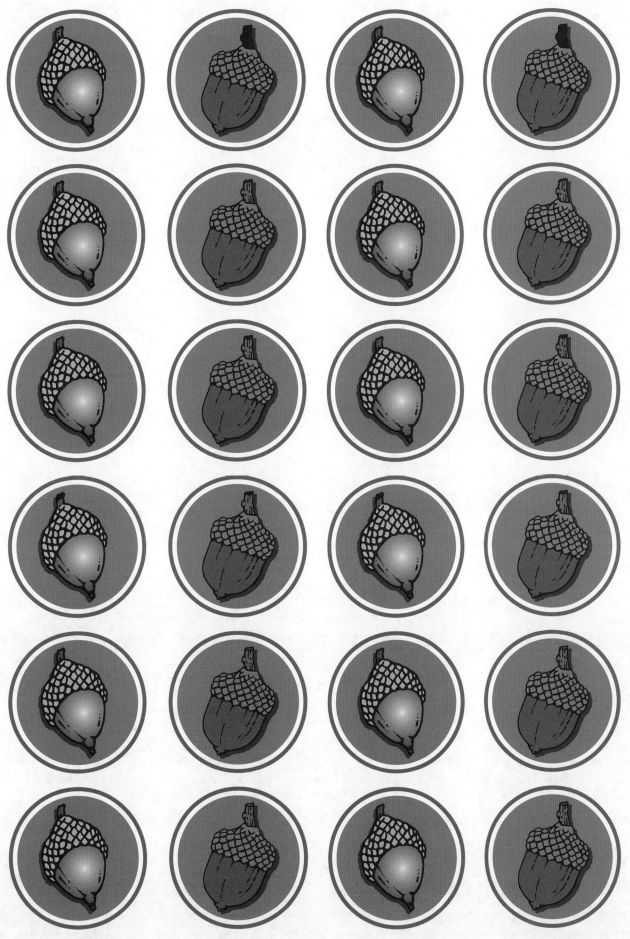

Redwood Racket

Rhyming Sounds

Objective: To identify rhyming sounds.

Preparation

1. Assemble and laminate the Redwood Racket Game Board (pages 134 and 135).

2. Laminate and cut out the Redwood Racket Rhyming Picture Cards (pages 137, 139, and 141).

3. Laminate and cut out the Woodpecker Cover Ups (page 143).

4. Laminate the Redwood Racket Directions Card (page 131).

5. Store the Redwood Racket Rhyming Picture Cards and Woodpecker Cover Ups in a resealable snack bag. Label the bag with the game name label (page 175).

6. See page 176 for the correct picture card names.

Redwood Racket Directions

Materials

- Redwood Racket Game Board
- Redwood Racket Rhyming Picture Cards
- Woodpecker Cover Ups

How to Play the Game

2–4 players

1. Shuffle the rhyming picture cards and place them facedown beside the game board.

2. Divide the Woodpecker Cover Ups among the players.

3. Take turns drawing a rhyming picture card and covering the matching rhyming picture on the game board with a cover up.

4. Continue taking turns until all the rhyming pictures on the game board have been covered.

REDWOOD RACKET

Rhyming Picture Cards

Redwood

Racket

Redwood

Racket

Redwood

Racket

Redwood

Racket

Redwood

Racket

Redwood

Racket

Redwood

Racket

Redwood

Racket

Rhyming Picture Cards

Redwood
Racket

Redwood
Racket

Redwood
Racket

Redwood
Racket

Redwood
Racket

Redwood
Racket

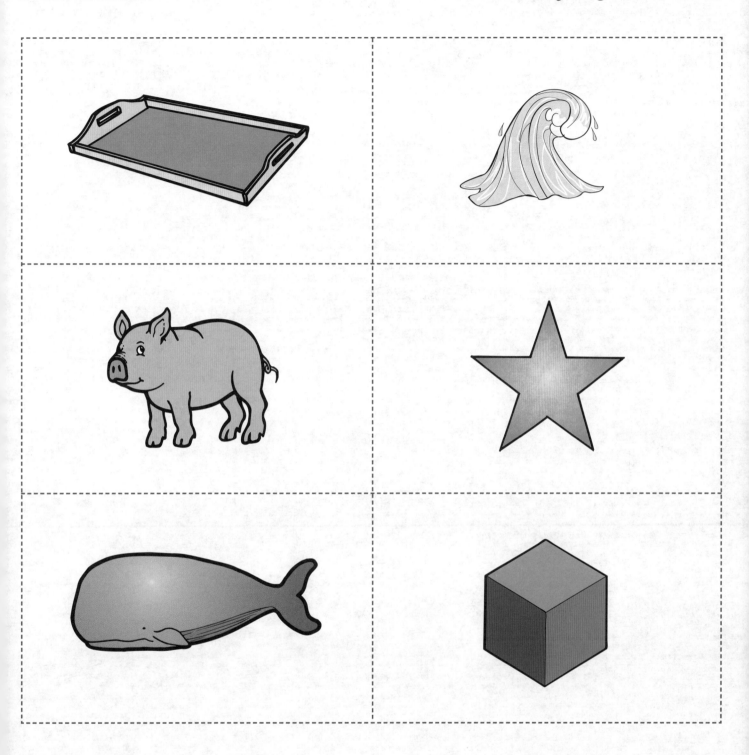

Rhyming Picture Cards

Redwood

Racket

Redwood

Racket

Redwood

Racket

Redwood

Racket

Redwood

Racket

Redwood

Racket

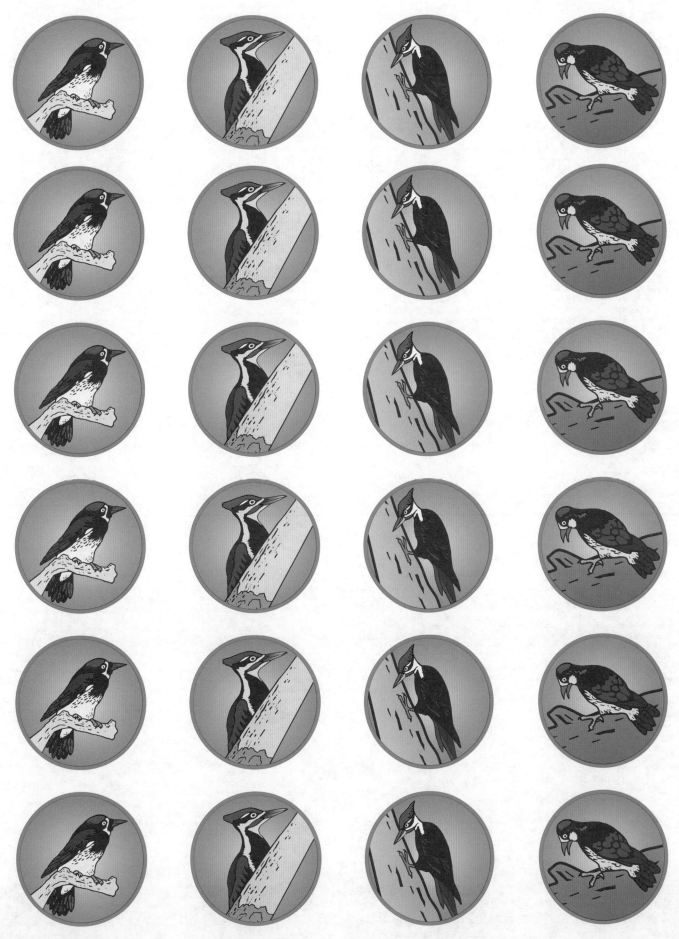

Palm Paradise

Rhyming Sounds

Objective: To identify rhyming sounds.

Preparation

1. Assemble and laminate the Palm Paradise Game Board (pages 148 and 149).

2. Laminate and cut out the Palm Paradise Rhyming Picture Cards (pages 151, 153, and 155).

3. Laminate and cut out the Coconut Cover Ups (page 157).

4. Laminate the Palm Paradise Directions Card (page 145).

5. Store the Palm Paradise Rhyming Picture Cards and Coconut Cover Ups in a resealable snack bag. Label the bag with the game name label (page 175).

6. See page 176 for the correct picture card names.

Palm Paradise Directions

Materials

- Palm Paradise Game Board
- Palm Paradise Rhyming Picture Cards
- Coconut Cover Ups

How to Play the Game

2–4 players

1. Shuffle the rhyming picture cards and place them facedown beside the game board.

2. Divide the Coconut Cover Ups among the players.

3. Take turns drawing a rhyming picture card and covering the matching rhyming picture on the game board with a cover up.

4. Continue taking turns until all the rhyming pictures on the game board have been covered.

PALM PARA

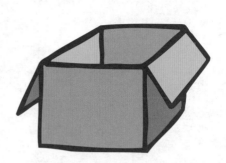

Rhyming Picture Cards

Palm

Paradise

Palm

Paradise

Palm

Paradise

Palm

Paradise

Palm

Paradise

Palm

Paradise

Palm

Paradise

Palm

Paradise

Rhyming Picture Cards

Palm
Paradise

Palm
Paradise

Palm
Paradise

Palm
Paradise

Palm
Paradise

Palm
Paradise

Rhyming Picture Cards

Palm
Paradise

Palm
Paradise

Palm
Paradise

Palm
Paradise

Palm
Paradise

Palm
Paradise

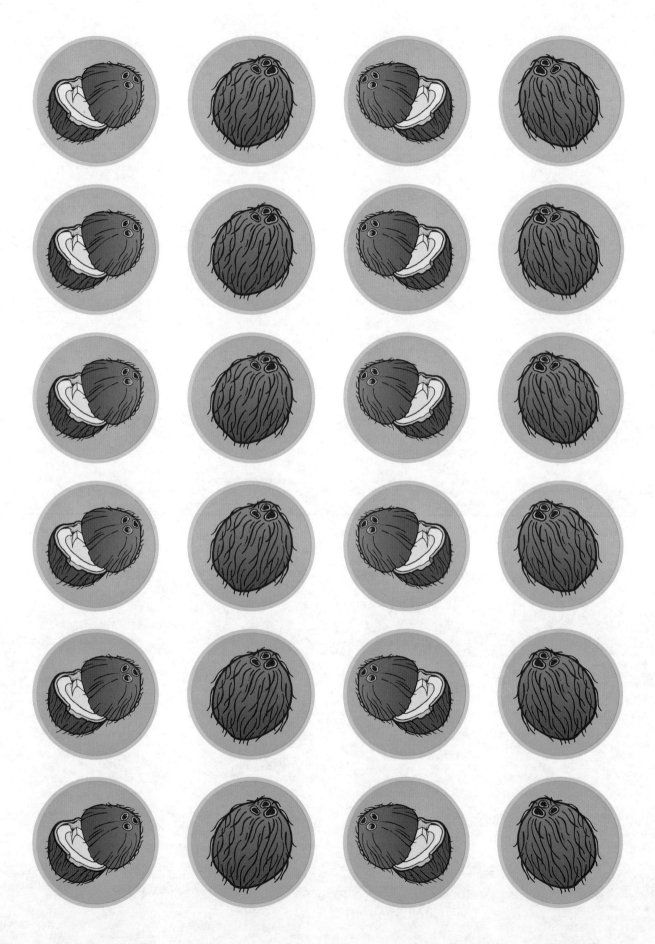

Outstanding Oranges

Rhyming Sounds

Objective: To identify rhyming sounds.

Preparation

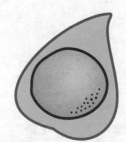

1. Assemble and laminate the Outstanding Oranges Game Board (pages 162 and 163).

2. Laminate and cut out the Outstanding Oranges Rhyming Picture Cards (pages 165, 167, and 169).

3. Laminate and cut out the Orange Cover Ups (page 171).

4. Laminate the Outstanding Oranges Directions Card (page 159).

5. Store the Outstanding Oranges Rhyming Picture Cards and Orange Cover Ups in a resealable snack bag. Label the bag with the game name label (page 175).

6. See page 176 for the correct picture card names.

Outstanding Oranges Directions

Materials

- Outstanding Oranges Game Board

- Outstanding Oranges Rhyming Picture Cards

- Orange Cover Ups

How to Play the Game

2–4 players

1. Shuffle the rhyming picture cards and place them facedown beside the game board.

2. Divide the Orange Cover Ups among the players.

3. Take turns drawing a rhyming picture card and covering the matching rhyming picture on the game board with a cover up.

4. Continue taking turns until all the rhyming pictures on the game board have been covered.

Outstanding Oranges

Outstanding Oranges

Outstanding Oranges

Outstanding Oranges

Outstanding Oranges

Outstanding Oranges

Outstanding Oranges

Outstanding Oranges

Rhyming Picture Cards

Outstanding Oranges

Outstanding Oranges

Outstanding Oranges

Outstanding Oranges

Outstanding Oranges

Outstanding Oranges

Rhyming Picture Cards

Outstanding Oranges

Outstanding Oranges

Outstanding Oranges

Outstanding Oranges

Outstanding Oranges

Outstanding Oranges

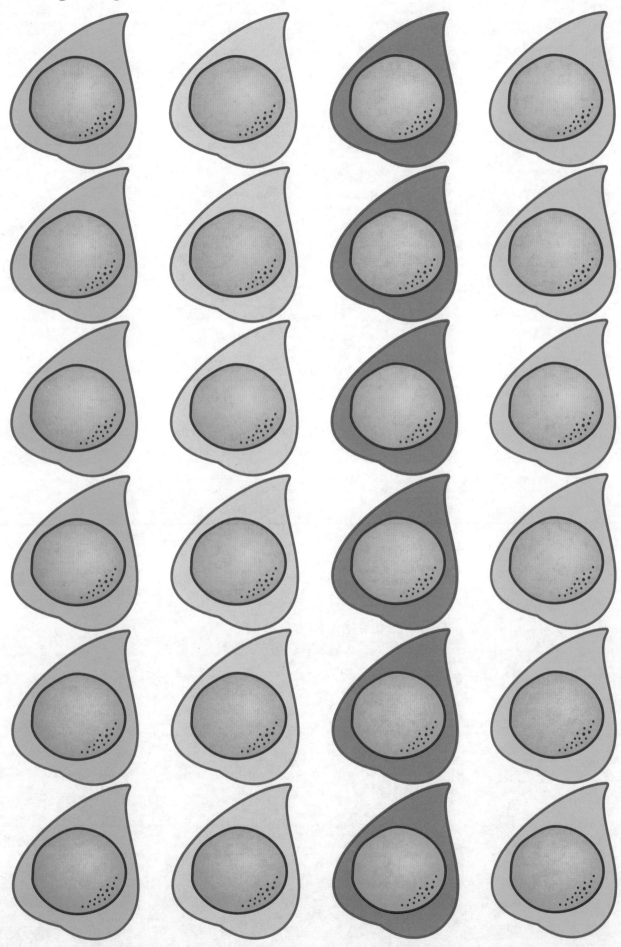

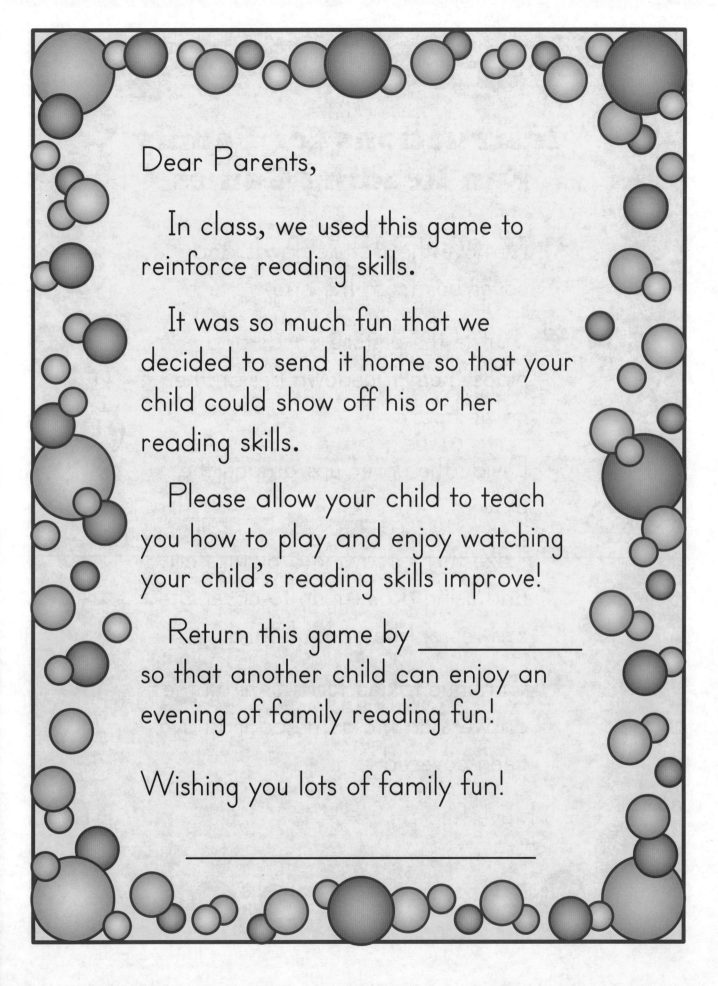

Dear Parents,

In class, we used this game to reinforce reading skills.

It was so much fun that we decided to send it home so that your child could show off his or her reading skills.

Please allow your child to teach you how to play and enjoy watching your child's reading skills improve!

Return this game by _____ so that another child can enjoy an evening of family reading fun!

Wishing you lots of family fun!

_____

Instructions for Family Fun Reading Games

♥ Remove the picture cards and cover ups from the bag.

♥ Shuffle the picture cards and place them facedown beside the game board.

♥ Divide the cover ups among the players.

♥ Take turns drawing a picture card and using a cover up to cover the answer on the game board.

♥ Continue taking turns until all the answers on the game board have been covered.

Have fun!

Game Labels

Dinosaur Days

Rusty the Rattler

Cool Chameleons

Lazy Lizards

Wacky Wind

Weather Map

Swirling Snowflakes

Cottony Clouds

Old Oak

Redwood Racket

Palm Paradise

Outstanding Oranges

	Page 11 – can, map, ax, lamp, bed, ten, bell, net Page 13 – bib, fish, six, milk, fox, dog Page 15 – sock, top, bus, gum, sun, rug
	Page 25 – ant, hand, jam, fan, egg, nest, desk, feather Page 27 – crib, ship, pig, kitten, box, mop Page 29 – rock, lock, tub, drum, mug, nut
	Page 39 – ham, van, bat, flag, leg, pen, red, vest Page 41 – pin, wig, mitt, lip, frog, block Page 43 – ox, pot, duck, bug, puppy, brush
	Page 53 – gas, tag, stamp, trap, well, dress, sled, bread Page 55 – dig, dish, fin, mitten, clock, stop Page 57 – log, dots, up, truck, skunk, cut
	Page 67 – snake, rain, wave, nail, bee, jeep, leaf, feet Page 69 – bike, hive, fire, kite, boat, soap Page 71 – bone, rose, uniform, flute, cube, mule
	Page 81 – rake, train, vase, snail, knee, tree, queen, sheet Page 83 – five, nine, bride, tire, rope, coat Page 85 – hose, cone, music, unicorn, ruler, suit
	Page 95 – cake, cane, mail, tape, green, deer, seal, meat Page 97 – vine, slide, light (bulb), tie, goat, robe Page 99 – flag pole, toad, ruler, fruit, uniform, music
	Page 109 – game, cave, tray, chain, cheese, read, three, key Page 111 – dime, pie, dive, lion, road, goal Page 113 – bow, globe, glue, tube, ukelele, unicycle
	Page 123 – jeep, house, map, flag, net, ten, fish, knight Page 125 – blue, dime, fan, feet, key, mail Page 127 – hose, nurse, money, bell, chain, road
	Page 137 – bat, pink, nickel, zoo, tag, key, ship, slide Page 139 – sun, lock, dog, cane, swing, goat Page 141 – tray, wave, pig, star, whale, cube
	Page 151 – mitten, box, log, stop, red, car, king, bell Page 153 – goat, duck, map, tree, drum, sock Page 155 – crib, bone, fire, bug, van, jam
	Page 165 – well, door, five, green, chick, book, snail, spoon Page 167 – stamp, vest, sled, egg, star, snake Page 169 – skate, tie, train, cape, lock, soap